rian's Brilliant
Career

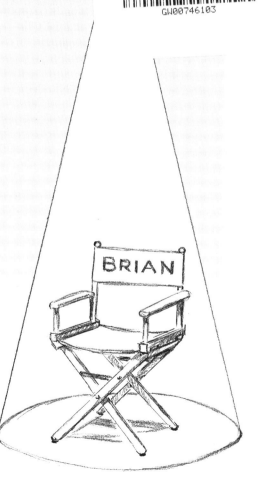

BRIAN

Written by Pamela Rushby
Illustrated by Liz Dodson

© 1995 Shortland Publications

07 06 05 04 03 02
12 11 10 9 8 7 6 5

Published by Shortland Publications

Distributed in New Zealand by Shortland Publications,
10 Cawley St, Ellerslie, Auckland, New Zealand
Distributed in Australia by Rigby Heinemann,
a division of Reed International Books Australia Pty Ltd.
ACN 001 002 357, 22 Salmon Street, Port Melbourne, Victoria 3207
Distributed in the United Kingdom by Kingscourt/McGraw-Hill
Shoppenhangers Road, Maidenhead, Berkshire SL6 2QL

Printed in China through Bookbuilders

ISBN: 0-7901-1074-1

Contents

Chapter 1

My "Brilliant Career" began when a television news crew visited my school. My school had a special environmental project for the year, working on cleaning up and replanting a swampy section down behind the railway, and some television people wanted to film us working on it for a programme they were making on environmental issues.

It just so happened that my class was working there the afternoon the television crew came. Some kids were clearing weeds, some were planting little trees, and I was up to my knees in mud, collecting rubbish that'd been tipped into the mud over the years. Some of it was pretty gross – old tyres, tin cans, plastic bottles, and some things that were absolutely unidentifiable, and that I preferred not to think about.

I was feeling totally disgusted with the people who'd thrown all this stuff into the swamp. So when all of a sudden this television crew showed up, someone pointed a camera at me, someone else held a microphone on a long pole over my head, and the reporter asked what I thought about my clean-up contribution to the project, I let them have it.

I told them just what I thought about people who dropped rubbish all over the place because they couldn't be bothered taking it to the tip. I pointed out all the disgusting stuff I'd already

pulled out of the swamp. I explained the harm it was doing to the wildlife in the area. I gave them a brief run-down on what it'd already done to the trees and plants. I flung my arms out for emphasis, and told them how wonderful it'd be when we had got it all tidied up. Then I slipped, stumbled, and fell flat on my face in the mud.

The kids in my class just loved it. The television crew did, too. I could see them coming in for a close-up as I wiped the mud out of my eyes. Even the principal was having trouble keeping a straight face – and normally, his face is so straight you could use it as a ruler. The only one who wasn't having a good time was me. I crawled out of the mud and went off to the boys' toilets to clean up.

Cleaning up took me quite awhile. When I came out, still muddy, the television crew was packing up. One of them, a woman, was waiting outside the toilet for me.

"That was quite a performance you gave there," she said.

I'd taken about as much as I could for one day. "Yeah," I said. "I'm just great at falling flat on my face in a swamp."

"No, I mean it," she insisted. "Your piece to camera was great."

I must have looked blank.

"Your piece to camera," she repeated, then went on to explain. "The talk you gave us about what you were doing, and what you thought about it. You did it really well. Have you done any on-camera work before?"

I looked even blanker. I shook my head. A slithery bit of swamp slime dropped out of my hair.

The woman laughed. "Look," she said, "this obviously isn't a good time to talk. My name's Julie. When I'm not working with this television station, I do some work for a casting agency – a place that supplies actors for television shows and commercials. I liked the way you talked to the camera this afternoon. It looked good. You looked good." She grinned. "Well, you did until you fell over." She reached into her pocket and pulled out a little, white business card. "Here, take this. Give it to your mum and dad. Ask them to give me a ring. There might, just might, be some work for you."

I took the card and glanced at it. I wasn't quite sure what she was talking about. Then the bell rang. I put the card in my shirt pocket, and forgot all about it.

I forgot about it until a few days later. It was after school. Mum was home from work, and catching up on some ironing. My younger sister, Fliss, and I were watching TV.

I heard Mum come out from the laundry. She was holding a messy, little bit of white paper in her hand.

"Brian, how many times have I told you not to leave things in the pockets of your school shirts?" she demanded. "Look at this! It's been through the washing machine, and the drier, too, and now I've ironed it. I haven't got a clue what it is. Is it your bus pass again?"

"No. That's blue," I said. I took the crumpled bit of paper from her, pried it open, and looked at it. I couldn't make out what it was at first. Then I remembered.

"Oh, it's a phone number," I said. "The woman from the television crew gave it to me. You know, the ones that filmed us at school. She wanted you or Dad to ring her."

"What for?" said Mum.

"What'd you do?" said Fliss. I could see she hoped it was something awful.

"Nothing!" I said indignantly. "I don't know what it's about. She said something about maybe having some work for me."

Mum took the card back and looked at it closely. "Brian, this is a casting agency," she said. "Did the woman talk about television work? Like modelling? Commercials?"

"Ahhhh," I said. "Don't know. Didn't ask."

"Oh, Brian!" said Mum, exasperated. "I think I'd better ring this person and see what it was all about."

"You? On TV?" said Fliss. "Not a chance! They only use good-looking people in commercials."

"Felicity!" said Mum warningly, on her way out the door.

Fliss and I made faces at each other. "Get lost," I said. I turned back to the TV show. I wasn't really interested in the whole thing.

But Mum and Dad were. Mum must have made the phone call, because soon after Dad got home, they came to talk to me. They were both looking at me in a funny way.

"Brian, this Julie person..." said Mum. "She wants us to bring you into the casting agency. She says she really thinks you might do well on television." Mum sounded as if she couldn't quite believe it.

Well, I hadn't really been interested in any of this at all. But now I was getting a bit offended. It wasn't as if I was *that* bad-looking. Yet here was my own mother acting as if my face would crack cameras. Dad gave me a look. Dad can always tell how I'm feeling.

"And why shouldn't Brian be good on television?" he said heartily. "Not a bad-looking boy, our Brian. Gets it from me, of course. Along with his charm, style, and impeccable manners – "

"And his modesty," said Mum. She was smiling by now. Dad can always make her laugh. "Well, it's your day off tomorrow, isn't it? Shall we take Brian to the agency in the afternoon and see what they say?"

"Do I get to miss school?" I said hopefully. It was worth a try.

"After school," said Mum firmly. Just as I'd expected.

"You mean you're really going to take him?" said Fliss. "Can I come?"

"No," I said.

"Maybe," said Mum.

"Why not?" said Dad.

So, of course, Fliss came.

Chapter 2

The casting agency was a very glossy-looking place. The foyer had big, soft leather settees, enough huge pot plants to stock the average rain forest, and a shiny, black marble floor. There were pictures of people on the walls. We recognized some of them. We'd seen them on television.

When Julie came out to meet us, even she looked glossy. Working with the crew, at school, she'd worn jeans and a jersey. Now she was all dressed up. But the smile was the same.

"Hello, Brian!" she said. "Glad you could make it!" Then she turned to Mum and Dad. She wanted a few of the agency people to see me first, she said. Then they'd probably want to put me on camera, just to see how I looked. If that all went OK, I could be entered on the agency's books, and the agency would try to find work for me.

That would mean, said Julie, that I'd have to get some photographs taken and printed, so that the agency could show them to people who might be interested in having me appear in their commercials. We'd have to pay for the photographs.

I saw Mum and Dad exchange a look. Money? that look said. How much money? Is this a rip-off of some sort?

Julie saw the look, too. "It's entirely up to you," she said. "We do have to have the photographs. I'll be quite honest with you. This is a reputable agency, and I really think we can get Brian some work, but, of course, we can't guarantee it. When everyone's seen Brian, and we've made our decision, it'll be up to you to decide whether you want to go ahead or not."

Mum and Dad looked a bit happier.

"Are you all right, Brian?" said Julie.

"Should we come?" said Mum.

"Probably better if you don't," said Julie. "It might make Brian self-conscious, having you there.

What do you think, Brian?"

I looked at Fliss. I could just imagine her watching. "I'll be fine," I said.

And then things moved very, very fast. Julie and I went into a corridor with office doors opening off it. Julie hurried along, popping her head into doorways and calling people's names.

"Harry? Got five minutes? Conference room."

"Sal? Conference room."

"Lisa? Possible new talent. Conference room."

The conference room was at the end of the corridor. By the time we reached it, there were six people following us. We went into the conference room, Julie gave me a chair, and I sat down. And everyone looked at me. Every so often, someone would say "Hmmm." Then they'd all move about and find a different angle. Then they'd all look at me again.

It was really embarrassing. After a few minutes, I could feel my face starting to get hot. It always does that when I get embarrassed. I can never stop it. I tried to think of cool things, like ice-cream, and the public swimming pool. The freezer in the fridge. Antarctica. I thought how glad I was Fliss

hadn't been allowed in. But it was no good. I felt my face getting warmer and warmer. Even my ears felt as if they were burning.

At last Julie noticed. "Oh, Brian, you poor thing!" she exclaimed. "Here, have a drink!" She rushed over to a little fridge, put lots of ice into a glass, poured in some orange juice, and handed it to me. I took a big, cold mouthful and relaxed a bit.

Everyone else relaxed, too. They all sat down and started asking me questions. School, where I lived, what I did at weekends, whether I'd always wanted to work on TV – that sort of thing. Soon I was quite comfortable again, and talking just as hard as they'd let me.

Harry asked if it'd bother me if they put a camera on me. It did, of course, because I could see there was a television set (only they called it a monitor) in the corner, and some of them watched me on that, while one or two of them talked to me. But I've never really been stuck for words (Dad says I could talk under wet concrete), so I just went along with it.

After awhile, they turned the camera off, and all got into a little group and talked to each other.

Then Julie took me back to the foyer. Fliss was looking pretty bored by now, just hanging about with no one paying her any attention. Serves her right, I thought. She had to come.

Julie sat down and smiled at Mum and Dad. "Well, we'd certainly like to have Brian on our books," she said. "He comes up very well on camera. Very animated. Lots of personality. How do you feel about it?"

Mum and Dad exchanged a look. "I think we'd like to talk it over," said Dad.

"Of course," said Julie. "You've got my number. Let me know when you've decided."

Chapter 3

It was a quiet drive home. Mum and Dad kept looking at me as if they'd never seen me before.

We stopped at a hamburger place for tea, and they were so preoccupied that Fliss and I managed to order two superburgers, a giant-sized shake, big chips, and a sundae each. Usually we'd never get away with that. We started eating quickly, hoping they wouldn't notice.

"Well," said Dad at last, sipping his coffee, "what do you reckon, Brian? Do you want to do it?"

I'd thought about it in the car. It could be fun. But would it get in the way of basketball and a few other things I wanted to do? On the other hand, I'd get paid, wouldn't I? That was definitely a major plus! While I thought, I started on my sundae. I managed to get a blob of the chocolate sauce on the end of my nose. So I did my party trick – about the only trick I can do. I try to look like I'm a lizard. I crossed my eyes and stared at the blob of chocolate, then slid out a long, slow lizard tongue and, all of a sudden, flashed out my tongue and licked it off.

Mum grinned at me. My lizard trick always gives her a laugh.

"So what do you reckon, Brian?" said Dad patiently.

"I wouldn't mind giving it a go," I said.

"It's like this," said Mum. "Julie said the photos would cost a couple of hundred dollars." Fliss and I stared. THAT much?

"We're willing to pay for the photos," Mum went on, "if you really want to do it. But if you're half-hearted about it, you won't try hard, and you won't get any jobs, and it'd be a waste of money. So – "

"Who in their right mind would give Brian a job in a TV commercial?" hooted Fliss. "You have to be good-looking!"

Mum and Dad frowned at her. "Felicity!" they said.

And that settled it for me. I was going to do it. I'd try my hardest to get a few jobs. Just to show Fliss!

I made a face at her. "I'd like to do it," I said firmly.

"Right," said Dad. "We know you'll do your best." Then he looked around at the pile of wrapping on the table. "Was someone here before us? A troop of Boy Scouts or something? Just how much did you two eat?" he demanded. Fliss and I scooped up the last of our sundaes and grinned at him.

Chapter 4

Mum and I went to the casting agency one afternoon and had the photos taken. I watched Mum as she wrote out the cheque. I could see she was thinking of quite a few things that couple of hundred dollars would have bought. For the first time, I was worried. I was in this up to my neck now. What if I didn't get any jobs? That couple of hundred dollars would be right down the drain.

For awhile it looked as if that's just where it was. A couple of weeks went by. The casting agency didn't ring. Mum and Dad kept giving me sympathetic looks. Fliss's were rather different. She didn't come right out and say "Told you so," but she might as well have.

Then I came home one afternoon after

basketball practice. "There was a phone call for you," said Fliss. "From the casting agency. They want you to call back." It had almost choked her to say it, but she'd got it out.

I called back straightaway, my insides churning. Could it be a job? Please let it be a job!

It wasn't quite a job. It was an audition, Julie said. An advertising agency was making a commercial for a new kind of ice-cream, and they were looking at quite a few kids. She'd suggested me. She gave me the address for the audition, and the time I had to be there, and said "Good luck!" encouragingly.

So a couple of days later, there I was, wandering up and down the footpath outside the advertising agency, trying to get up enough courage to go in. Mum and Dad hadn't been able to take time off work to come with me, and I'd told them I'd be fine by myself. I knew Julie would be coming along later, to see whether any of her agency's kids had got the job, but at the moment, I was on my own. And I didn't like it.

I stared and stared at the building and thought about going home. Did I really want to do this?

"Here for the audition?" said someone behind me. I turned around. It was a girl about my age, in jeans and a T-shirt and a hat with a turned-back brim and a daisy pinned on it. She looked familiar somehow.

"Is it your first audition?" she said.

"It's that obvious, eh?" I asked.

She grinned and nodded. "Just a bit," she said. "It's scary, going in by yourself, isn't it? C'mon.

Come with me."

The girl really knew what to do. She went confidently up the steps and in the door, and called "Hello, Lisa!" to the girl at the reception desk.

"Hi, Evvie!" the girl replied. "The audition's in the boardroom. You know the way." Evvie went on up a big flight of steps, dragging me behind her.

There were about ten kids sitting in a waiting area outside the boardroom. All ages, all kinds of looks. Black, white, Chinese. Some of the younger ones had a mum or dad with them.

"Hmmm," said Evvie, looking at them. "Real mixture. It either means the agency people haven't made up their minds what they want, or they're going to use a crowd."

"You've made commercials before?" I asked.

"Mmmm," she said. "A few. Biscuits. Dog food. Fizzy drinks."

Then I knew why she looked so familiar. She hadn't made a few commercials. She'd made a lot. I'd seen her on TV, just last week, in a dog food commercial. She was feeding a group of really big dogs, St. Bernards, and they pushed her over, and she sat in the middle of them, holding the tin up

and saying "They really love it!" while the dogs licked her face.

"Was that you?" I said. "In the dog food commercial? That must have been fun! They're incredible dogs!"

She nodded, a bit grimly. "They've got incredible licks, too," she said. "I was covered in dog slobber. Doing commercials isn't as much fun as it looks at times. Especially with dogs."

"But this is ice-cream!" I said. "It'll be great!"

Evvie wasn't convinced. "Ice-cream has its drawbacks, too," she said.

I couldn't imagine what they could be. Eating ice-cream? Being paid to do it? Where was the catch? But I didn't have time to ask, because a girl with a clipboard came out and called me into the boardroom. "Brian? Brian – come on in, please."

I froze. Absolutely froze. My knees were actually

shaking as I got up. Evvie glanced at me and grabbed my arm. She pulled me down to whisper in my ear.

"Wait a minute!" she hissed. "If you go in there shaking and twitching and being shy, you'll never get the job. Don't let 'em see that you're nervous. Let 'em see how great you are! *Project!*" And she gave me a big smile.

She was right, I knew. So I stood up straight, took a deep breath, pretended everything was cool, and strolled into the boardroom, following the girl with the clipboard. I glanced back at Evvie. She grinned, winked, and gave me a thumbs-up. I grinned back.

There were three or four people in the room, sitting behind a big desk, and they all looked at me. And looked. And looked. Keep cool! I told myself. It's just like going to the casting agency for the first time! I gave them a big, confident grin.

"Brian?" said one man, looking at a list. "Mmmm. Brian. Do you like ice-cream?"

"Well, of course," I said. They seemed to be waiting for more. I told myself, *Project*, Brian. I took a deep breath. "I love ice-cream!" I said. "Just

LOVE it! It's my favourite food. I like chocolate best – especially chocolate coated in chocolate. Dark chocolate, preferably – " I prattled on and on. I was starting to run out of things to say. I mean, how much is there to say about ice-cream, no matter how much you like it? I was delighted when they stopped me.

"Just eat that for us, will you?" Another man was passing me an ice-cream bar. I didn't need to be asked twice.

"Sure!" I said. I took a bite. "Mmmm! Great!" But have you ever tried eating an ice-cream bar with four people watching every bite you take? It's not easy. I tried to eat tidily, which is not the way to enjoy ice-cream. And you know how chocolate coating cracks, and bits fall off? This ice-cream bar was no different. Suddenly, a bit of the chocolate coating snapped, flipped up, and hit me in the face. From the corner of my eye, I could see it had left a blob of ice-cream right on the end of my nose.

Disaster! Or just maybe it needn't be. *Project*! I told myself. And I did my party trick: crossed my eyes, stared at the blob of ice-cream, slid out a slow lizard tongue, then – flash! I zapped out my tongue, and licked the blob of ice-cream off, and smiled triumphantly at them.

They loved it. They all laughed. One of them noted something on his list. "I don't think we need to see any more from him, do you?" he said to the others. "That's it, then, Brian. We'll be in touch. You can go now."

"What do I do with the ice-cream?" I asked.

"It's yours," the man grinned. "Enjoy it."

On my way out, with the dripping ice-cream bar in my hand, I met Evvie on her way in.

"How'd it go?" she whispered.

I grinned at her. "I *projected*!" I said.

Chapter 5

I knew the audition had gone pretty well. But somehow, I didn't really expect to get the job. Not with people like Evvie there, people who made commercials all the time.

So when Mum answered the phone that evening and said, "Oh, hello, Julie," and then, "He DID?" I was really surprised. Pleased, but surprised. And suddenly very, very nervous. I was beginning to suspect that there was more to making commercials than I'd thought. And, in fact, there was. A lot, lot more.

I found out just how much more when I turned up for my first job, the ice-cream commercial. It was being shot in a studio near the city. The area we were using was a big, bare room with three cameras

set up at one end, a whole lot of other equipment, and a roll of blue paper hanging from the ceiling. I had to stand in front of the paper, take a big bite out of the ice-cream, and do my party trick.

The blue paper, they told me, was a sort of trick. Chroma-keying, it was called. Later on, they'd replace the blue paper background with some computer animation, and I'd look as if there was coloured steam coming out of my ears and bells ringing and butterflies and birds flying all around me, all because I liked the ice-cream so much.

"Yeah, right," I said. "Whatever you say."

But they weren't kidding. Someone gave me a touch of powder, someone else combed my hair, and I was given some clothes to wear. Nothing with blue in it, they explained, because that'd affect the chroma-keying process. And we started.

I was shown just where to stand on the blue paper, someone passed me an ice-cream bar from a huge fridge, and the director called "Action!" I opened my mouth wide. The first bite of ice-cream was great.

"Let's try it again," said the director.

I got ready to take a second bite.

"No, no," said the production assistant. "New ice-cream, Brian. We're doing another take – taking it from the top again. That means the ice-cream bar has to be a new one." She took the ice-cream bar with the bite out of it from my hand and threw it into a rubbish bin. What a waste! I thought. Then she looked at me. "Did you swallow that bite?" she asked.

"Well, yeah," I said. I wondered what else she thought I'd do with it.

"Don't, next time," she advised. "Spit it out. Otherwise, you'll be pretty sick of ice-cream by the end of the day."

Me? Sick of ice-cream? No way! That woman was crazy.

But by the end of the afternoon, I'd found she wasn't crazy at all. We'd shot that scene – me taking one bite, crossing my eyes, and licking the tip of my nose – about thirty times before the director was satisfied.

By take fifteen my eyes felt as if they were permanently crossed. And I was taking the production assistant's advice, and spitting the ice-cream out. But it was a bit late.

We did the scene for the thirty-first time. I slowly and painfully uncrossed my eyes. "Great!" called the director. "Well done, Brian! That's a wrap, folks!" I wasn't sure what a wrap was, but everyone else seemed to understand it was the end of the day. They started packing up.

I sat down, very carefully, and tried not to look at the melting ice-cream bars in the rubbish.

"You OK?" said the production assistant. "You look a bit green."

"Fine," I said. "Just fine."

The director came over. "Great stuff, Brian!" he said. He looked closer. "Are you OK?"

"Fine," I said. "Just fine."

"Often happens with ice-cream commercials," said the director cheerfully. "Chocolate, too. And biscuits. And – "

I didn't want to think about it. I was very pleased when Dad arrived to pick me up.

"Well, how does fame and fortune feel?" said Dad heartily.

"Fine," I said. "Just fine."

Chapter 6

I rode home with my eyes shut, feeling very nervous every time the car swung sharply around a corner. I didn't want any tea. I went straight to bed. If this is fame and fortune, I thought, keeping my head very still on the pillow, I don't think I want any more of it.

But of course, when my payment cheque arrived a week or so later, I'd forgotten how sick I'd felt. I just felt rich. I stared at the cheque. Wow! Fame? Fortune? I definitely wanted more! Well, more fortune, anyway – even though Mum and Dad made me put most of the money I'd earned into my bank account.

So, a couple of weeks later when Julie phoned again, I was keen and ready to go.

"It's a commercial for a big department store," said Julie. "A new range of boys' clothing. Very trendy and expensive, I believe, from Italy."

"Is the audition at the same place?" I asked.

Julie laughed. "You're becoming famous," she said. "The department store people saw the edit of the ice-cream commercial. They decided you were just what they wanted. No audition necessary this time."

"Wow," I said, impressed.

Mum and Dad were busy on the day the commercial was to be shot, so Julie picked me up from school and took me to the studio. It was a different studio, and a much bigger production.

This time there was a real set, a sort of cartoon city street painted on the wall, and some props, cut-out cars, signposts, and letter-boxes standing around.

I didn't think much of the clothes. There were big, baggy shorts; pleated trousers; and shirts with wide, gathered sleeves. Even a bow tie. But the department store people said they were the very latest thing, and parents would be flocking to buy them.

There was also a real make-up person, who brushed my hair up on end and put on my make-up, and gave me some silly, little, circular sunglasses to wear.

And there was a choreographer, someone who showed me how to move to the music they'd be using. That was fun. He was an incredible dancer, and he taught me some of the latest dance steps. We were having a blast. Then the wardrobe manager called me in for the fitting.

In the dressing-room, I stepped out of my T-shirt and shorts. The make-up artist handed me the first outfit, waited for me to put it on, then tweaked and patted it into place. "That's it!" she said. "Ready!" I looked in the full-length mirror on the wall.

I wouldn't have known it was me. My own mother wouldn't have known it was me. But she would have liked it, I knew. I looked – different. Sharp. Cool. Trendy. Even the circular sun-glasses fitted right in.

I strolled out onto the set, sliding the sun-glasses casually down my nose and peering coolly over them. "Great!" said the director. "Keep that in. We'll use it."

The shoot moved a lot faster this time. I had to wear one of the outfits, and dance across the set until I got behind one of the props, the cut-out cars, or letter-boxes. Then they'd stop the camera, I'd change clothes, and dance out from behind the other side of the prop in the new outfit. We did each scene several times, first for the long shots and then again so they could shoot close-ups.

It was all going just great, until I went back to

the dressing-room for the last change of clothes. The make-up artist handed me a clothes-hanger with nothing on it but a little bit of bright red, shiny, satin fabric.

I waited. "Where's the rest?" I asked.

"That's it," said the make-up artist.

"But there must be more!" I protested.

"Well, I'll check with the department store people," she said. "But that's all that's on the hanger with that number."

She was back in a moment. "Yes," she said. "There is more. I'll find it."

That was a relief. Just for a moment, I'd been worried. I took the little bit of red satin off the hanger and shook it out. It was a pair of briefs. And when I say briefs, I mean BRIEF. They were barely there. Whew! I thought. I'm glad there's more.

"Here's the rest," said the make-up artist. She handed me a pair of socks. Bright red socks.

"That's IT?" I said. "Oh no. No way."

"There's not much to the outfit, is there?" agreed the make-up artist. "But it's OK. They said they wouldn't be filming your face for this shot. Just the underwear. No one'll ever know it's you."

Won't they? I thought.

The make-up artist looked at me. "It's the last outfit," she said, a bit anxiously. "Pop 'em on, Brian. Let's go!"

There was no way I was walking out into that roomful of people, wearing about ten square centimetres of red satin and a pair of socks – whether anyone was going to see my face or not.

"Not a chance," I said. I sat down and folded my arms. The make-up artist took one look at me and went to get Julie.

"Brian, I know they're about ten square centimetres," said Julie, as I waved the briefs accusingly at her. "I know it's embarrassing. I know you'd rather not do it. Believe me, I sympathize."

Does she mean I don't have to do it? I thought hopefully.

"BUT –" said Julie.

Nope, I thought. She doesn't mean I don't have to do it.

"BUT," said Julie. "There's a director, and a whole crew, and a lot of people from the department store out there, all waiting for you. What do I tell them? That you're embarrassed? You're a professional now, Brian. Professionals don't get embarrassed. You accepted the job. You have to do it."

I thought about it. I hated to admit it, but she was right. I wondered what Evvie would do. She'd *project!* I thought. Then I grinned. I doubted they'd have asked Evvie to appear in ten square centimetres of red satin. Or maybe Evvie would have had the sense to check the clothes first. I'd know better next time.

"OK, you win," I said. "Let's go."

"Good boy," said Julie, relieved. "And, Brian – don't let them see you're shy. Give it all you've got."

"*Project*?" I said.

"*Project*," said Julie.

So I gave it all I had. I danced across that set in those almost-not-there briefs and a pair of socks, just as I'd have done if I'd been covered modestly from neck to knee. The whole crew was laughing, but at least they were laughing with me, not at me. And they kept their word. They didn't film my face.

Chapter 7

Even though they didn't show my face in the underwear part of the ad, it didn't make the least bit of difference, of course. Everyone knew it was me. A few weeks later, Fliss shrieked from the lounge one evening, "Brian, it's your commercial! It's on TV!"

I knew the ice-cream commercial hadn't gone to air yet. It was scheduled for later in the summer. So it had to be the clothes. I groaned to myself.

Mum and Dad had rushed into the lounge to see it. Here it comes, I thought. I waited for the reactions.

"Hey, Brian," called Mum. "You look very... professional! I didn't know you could dance like that – like – like – oh, BRIAN!"

"Unbelievable!" said Dad. "Um, that wasn't really YOU, was it?"

Fliss was rolling on the floor, shrieking with laughter. "You bet it was!" she said. "Wait'll I tell the kids at school about THIS!"

"Mu-um!" I said.

Mum and Dad exchanged a look. "Felicity," said Dad firmly, "we'd like to talk to you."

But forbidding Fliss to talk about it at school didn't do any good either. I got a really bad time from the kids in my class the next day. Even a few of the teachers couldn't resist having a dig. Neither could the principal.

"Well, Brian," he said. "I saw you on TV last night. Very... interesting. Especially the underwear." He tried a joke, but he wasn't very good at it. Lack of practice, I suppose. "Will we be seeing a lot more of you in the future? Ha-ha!"

I looked him straight in the eye. "It was definitely a one-time appearance," I said.

It was a long, long day. By the end of it, I'd decided that this time, definitely, was the last. No more commercials. It just wasn't worth it. This was absolutely the end of my career.

Then, a couple of weeks later, Julie phoned up again.

"Nope," I said. "No way. Not a chance. Definitely not interested. Total apathy."

"Pity," said Julie. "It's a commercial for Easter eggs. They especially asked for you. And you remember Evvie, don't you? She's in it, too. But if you're really not interested, I suppose we could get someone else."

Evvie? Evvie was going to be in it? That changed things a bit.

"Um, this commercial," I said, carefully. "Easter eggs, you said? What would I have to wear?"

"Oh, it's really cute," said Julie. "Sort of Victorian. Pants, long pants, Brian, and a shirt with long sleeves and a few frills down the front."

Long pants. Long sleeves. Hmmm... No problem there. Frills? I could cope with a few frills, I thought.

"No underwear?" I said suspiciously.

"Definitely no underwear," said Julie.

Chapter 8

The commercial was being shot at the same studio where the department store commercial had been made. It was the same director and crew, too.

"Hi, Brian!" they called. "Nice to be working with you again!"

Much to my relief, no one mentioned the underwear.

I took a look at the set. It was like a garden, a spring garden, with flowers, a tiny fountain splashing real water, and a carved stone bench. The flowers were real – they'd brought in hundreds of pots, each with a plant blooming its head off. Tucked in among the flowers were Easter eggs wrapped in bright, shiny paper.

Sitting on the stone bench was a girl in a long, pink, frilly dress and a straw bonnet. Evvie!

"Hi, Brian!" she called.

She couldn't get up, because the crew was lighting the set and needed her in place, so I went over as close as I could, careful not to get in the crew's way.

"I heard you got the ice-cream commercial," said Evvie.

"Yeah," I said. "I did. And you were right. You can get really sick of ice-cream. Did you – I mean, did you mind? Did you really want to do that job?"

"Oh, win some, lose some," she said. "You never know who they're going to pick. Don't worry about it. It's everyone for themselves when you're after a job!"

"Yes, but you helped me," I said.

She looked surprised. "Did I? What'd I do?"

"Remember how you said I couldn't go in there looking shy, and you said '*Project*'? I did. I stopped being shy – well, I didn't actually stop, but I pretended I wasn't. And it worked."

Evvie grinned. "What'd you do?" she asked.

"This," I said. And I did my party trick.

Evvie nearly fell off the bench laughing. All the crew looked around, and laughed, too.

"He's at it again," said the production assistant, coming up behind us. "And fully clothed, too."

I blushed. I could feel it, starting at my neck and crawling up my face.

Evvie grinned at me. "I heard about the department store commercial, too," she said.

Boy, was I glad that the production assistant had suddenly appeared to take me away to get changed and made up!

Compared with the previous shoot, this one was a breeze. All we had to do was walk through the garden, finding Easter eggs among the flowers, and putting them into a straw basket I was carrying. We did it over and over, and then had to do the scene yet again for close-ups. Finally we broke for lunch.

I really liked the way they looked after you when a commercial was being shot. At a morning snack break, and at lunch-time, caterers brought in plenty of food and drinks, and everyone took a break.

The make-up artist covered Evvie and me up in big aprons so we couldn't get our costumes dirty, then told us to go and get something to eat. We talked to each other all through lunch.

We went to different schools, of course, but we found out that maybe we'd be going to the same intermediate school next year. We liked the same sort of music. I played basketball, and Evvie played netball. We both had a little sister, and we agreed that a younger sister could be a real pain. We were still talking when the director called everyone back onto the set.

"Right," he said. "Last shot. Stand right here, Evvie, there's your mark. OK, Brian, you're here. Now, when I say action, all you have to do is hand her the basket of eggs, and give her a kiss."

Silence.

"Give her a what?" I said.

"A kiss. Just a little peck on the lips. Right there. OK? Ready, everyone? Let's go!"

I stood quite still while the crew got into position. I didn't know why I'd questioned the director. I'd heard every word he said. Every word. And I knew I'd have to do it.

The director checked his shot in the monitor. "Hold it!" he said. "Make-up!" He turned to the make-up artist. "Brian's face is looking a bit hot. Tone him down a little, will you?"

I'd need a lot more than powder to tone me down, I thought, as the make-up person brushed away at my face. Deep breaths, Brian, I told myself. You can do it! *Project!*

"Action!" called the director.

But I couldn't do it. This was one time I just couldn't *project.*

I did my best. I handed Evvie the basket and I kissed her, right on the lips, just as I'd been told, but I knew I hadn't *projected.* I just knew I'd looked shy, bashful, and awkward. And there wasn't a thing I could do about it.

I stepped back, a mass of blushes. "Oh, boy, am I glad that's over," I thought.

"Mmmm," said the director, looking at the replay in his monitor. "Not bad, not bad. But we can do better. OK, folks, again please."

Again? Yes, indeed. And again. And again. And again...

And then we did the close-ups.

I didn't talk to Julie all the way home. My ears were still burning when she dropped me off and drove off with a cheerful wave. I walked into the lounge. Mum and Dad and Fliss were happily playing Monopoly.

"Hi, dear! How'd it go?" said Mum.

"Fine," I said. "Just fine."

"No underwear this time?" joked Dad.

"No underwear," I said.

Fliss looked up at me. "Do you know your ears are all red?" she said.

Chapter 9

When Julie called the next day, I was ready for her. This was definitely it. No more commercials, ever. Underwear's one thing. But there are some things you just can't ask a guy to do.

"I'm sorry you feel like that," said Julie. Was there a laugh in her voice? "The clients were thrilled to bits. They said you've got exactly the look they wanted – shy and sweet. They thought you were adorable. There could be a lot more work there. Wouldn't you like – "

"No way," I said. "Never again. Absolutely never."

"Never say never," said Julie. Definitely there was a laugh in her voice. "Why don't you think about it for awhile, Brian."

The ice-cream commercial had gone to air by now, but the kids at school hadn't given me any problems about it. It was sort of silly and funny, so no one had teased me. But this– I knew that as soon as they'd seen it, I was going to die.

I'd been told the date the Easter egg commercial would be going to air, but I'd kept it quiet. I didn't even tell Mum and Dad. I did my best to look pale and interesting the morning after it'd first been shown, so Mum would think I was sick and let me stay home from school. I didn't fool her for a minute. At 8:30 a.m., Mum dropped me off and there I was, walking into school, just the same as usual.

I headed straight for my classroom, and my desk. Maybe no one's seen the commercial yet, I thought hopefully. Maybe, just maybe. I put my books away in my desk, and kept my head down.

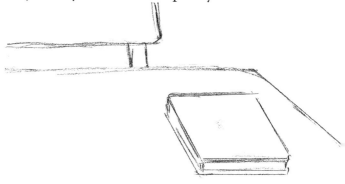

It was very quiet in the room, but suddenly I could feel people there. I looked up. There were at least eight kids around my desk, just standing there, looking at me. I braced myself. I waited for the teasing to start.

It was still very quiet. The kids shuffled their feet and glanced at each other. Then Maria Pappas poked Steve Mishinski in the back and made a face at him. "You go first," she hissed.

Steve hesitated. Then, "Did you really kiss her?" he said. "Really?"

My mouth fell open. The other kids broke in.

"Did you have to do it with everyone watching?"

"How many times did you do it?"

"Did they make you do it? Or was it your idea?"

"Was it really embarrassing?"

Then Bart Patterson, the biggest and toughest kid in the class, shoved his way to the front. He hesitated. Then, "Was it – gross?" he said.

And I just sat there and looked at them. Because it'd never occurred to me before. Sure, it'd been embarrassing. Sure, I hadn't wanted to do it. Sure, I'd never do it again. But to be perfectly honest, it hadn't been gross. No. It hadn't been gross at all.

So, I'm thinking about it. "Never say never," Julie had said. What will I do, I wonder, when she calls again. IF she calls again. Will I think about doing another commercial or two? Especially if Evvie's there! Or will I decide enough's enough, that this really is the end of my brilliant career?

It's a big decision.

TITLES IN THE SERIES